D1194118

LONGITUDE
AND LATITUDE

by Rebecca Olien

Content Consultant
Laura McCormick
Cartographer
XNR Productions Inc.

Children's Press®
An Imprint of Scholastic Inc.
New York Toronto London Auckland Sydney
Mexico City New Delhi Hong Kong
Danbury, Connecticut

Library of Congress Cataloging-in-Publication Data
Olien, Rebecca.
  Longitude and latitude/by Rebecca Olien.
    p. cm.—(Rookie read-about geography)
  Includes bibliographical references and index.
  ISBN-13: 978-0-531-28963-1 (lib. bdg.)   ISBN-13: 978-0-531-29287-7 (pbk.)
  1. Latitude—Juvenile literature. 2. Longitude—Juvenile literature. 3. Geographical
positions—Juvenile literature. I. Title.
  QB224.5.O45 2013
  526'.61—dc23   2012000510

SCHOLASTIC, CHILDREN'S PRESS, ROOKIE READ-ABOUT®, and associated logos
are trademarks and/or registered trademarks of Scholastic Inc.

1 2 3 4 5 6 7 8 9 10 R 22 21 20 19 18 17 16 15 14 13

Photographs © 2013: Getty Images/Victoria Blackie: 4; iStockphoto: 24 (btrenkel), 28,
29 top left (Christopher Futcher); Media Bakery/ULTRA.F: 6; Replogle Globes/www.
ReplogleGlobes.com: cover; Superstock, Inc./age fotostock: 18; The Image Works/
Eascott-Momatiuk: 26.

Maps by XNR Productions, Inc.

Table of Contents

Lines on a Map **5**

Side to Side **9**

Up and Down **13**

Lines on a Globe **19**

Follow the Lines **25**

Words You Know 29

Try It! 30

Facts for Now 31

Index 32

About the Author 32

4

Lines on a Map

Maps are flat and show drawings of places. Lines on a map help people find places.

People can look at the lines to see where something is located.

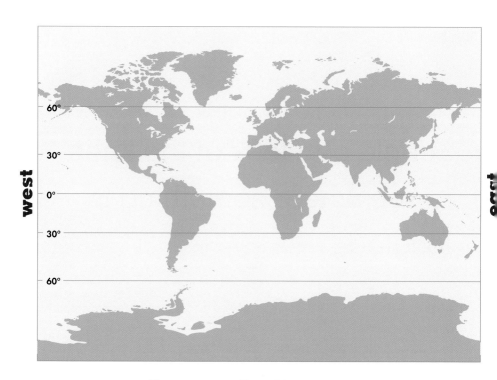

west

60°
30°
0°
30°
60°

latitude lines

Side to Side

Lines going across a map are latitude lines. They go from side to side. This is called east and west.

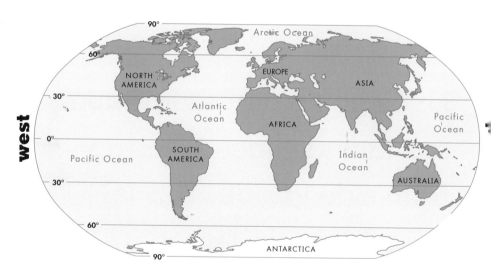

west

latitude lines

Follow a latitude line. Name one place you see.

north

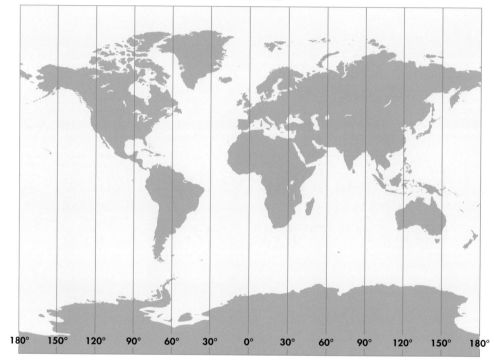

180° 150° 120° 90° 60° 30° 0° 30° 60° 90° 120° 150° 180°

south

longitude lines

12

Up and Down

Longitude lines go up and down. They run north and south on the map.

north

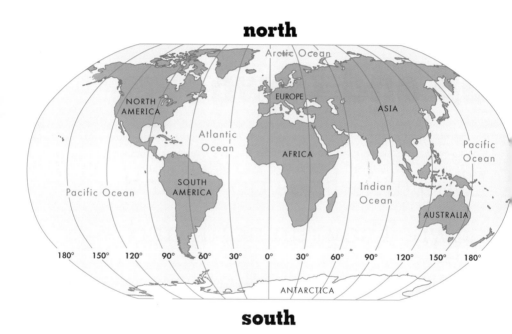

Arctic Ocean

NORTH
AMERICA

EUROPE

ASIA

Atlantic
Ocean

AFRICA

Pacific
Ocean

SOUTH
AMERICA

Indian
Ocean

Pacific Ocean

AUSTRALIA

180° 150° 120° 90° 60° 30° 0° 30° 60° 90° 120° 150° 180°

ANTARCTICA

south

longitude lines

14

Follow a longitude line down the map. Where do you go? Antarctica is at the bottom of the Earth. It is cold there. Brrr!

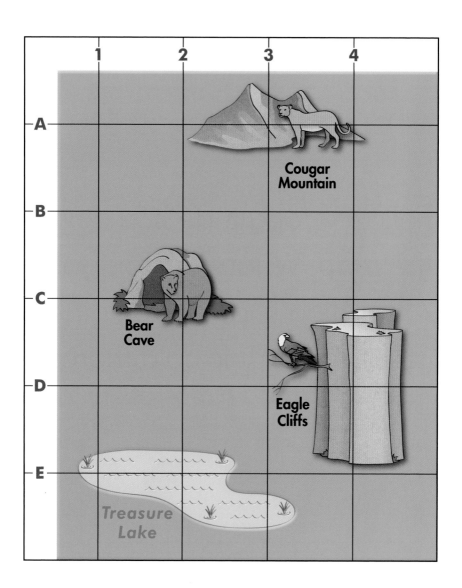

Longitude and latitude lines cross. They form a grid. A grid might be marked with letters and numbers. What do you see where lines C and 2 meet on this grid?

Lines on a Globe

A globe is in the shape of Earth. It is round like a ball. You can hold and spin a globe.

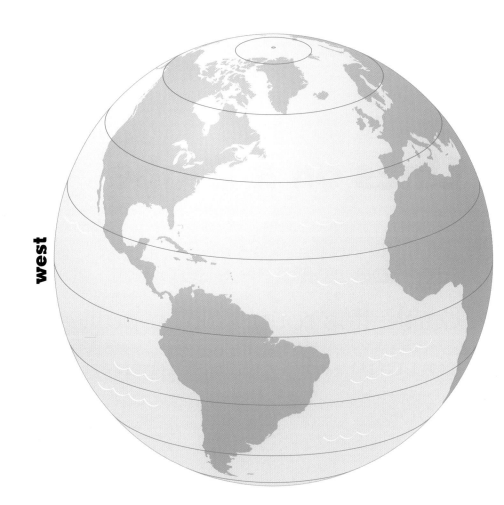

west

latitude lines

Latitude lines go around a globe.

north

south

longitude lines

Longitude lines go up and down.

Follow the Lines

The lines on maps and globes
help people find places.
People can follow the lines
to find a country or a city.

Sailors follow the lines to find where they are on the water. Pilots in the air use them, too.

Longitude and latitude
lines can help you, too.
Follow any line on a map
or a globe. What new
places do you find?

Words You Know

globe

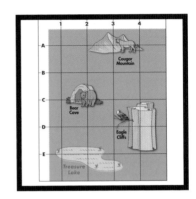

grid

latitude lines

longitude lines

TRY IT!

Look at this globe. Can you point to the latitude lines? Can you point to the longitude lines? The equator is a line that divides Earth in half. Where is the equator?

Visit this Scholastic Web site for
more information on longitude and latitude:
www.factsfornow.scholastic.com
Enter the keywords **Longitude and Latitude**

equator

31

Index

Antarctica, 15

cities, 25
countries, 25

east, 9

globes, 19, 21, 23, 25, 28
grids, 17

latitude, 9, 11, 17, 21, 27, 28
letters, 17

longitude, 13, 15, 17, 23, 27, 28

maps, 5, 9, 13, 15, 25, 28

north, 13
numbers, 17
pilots, 27

sailors, 27
south, 13

west, 9

About the Author

Rebecca Olien is a teacher and author of more than 50 books for educators and children. You can often find her studying maps to find new places to go.